Darell Reynolds

FAITH AND PROSPERITY Combine

104 Bi-Weekly Devotionals

WESTBOW
PRESS®
A DIVISION OF THOMAS NELSON
& ZONDERVAN

This book is a work of non-fiction. Unless otherwise noted, the author
and the publisher make no explicit guarantees as to the accuracy of
the information contained in this book and in some cases, names of
people and places have been altered to protect their privacy.

WestBow Press books may be ordered through booksellers or by contacting:

WestBow Press
A Division of Thomas Nelson & Zondervan
1663 Liberty Drive
Bloomington, IN 47403
www.westbowpress.com
1 (866) 928-1240

Because of the dynamic nature of the Internet, any web addresses or
links contained in this book may have changed since publication and
may no longer be valid. The views expressed in this work are solely those
of the author and do not necessarily reflect the views of the publisher,
and the publisher hereby disclaims any responsibility for them.

Any people depicted in stock imagery provided by Thinkstock are models,
and such images are being used for illustrative purposes only.
Certain stock imagery © Thinkstock.

ISBN: 978-1-5127-1027-4 (sc)
ISBN: 978-1-5127-1029-8 (hc)
ISBN: 978-1-5127-1028-1 (e)

Library of Congress Control Number: 2015914140

Print information available on the last page.

WestBow Press rev. date: 10/06/2015

CONTENTS

FOREWORD

I was once a different man, one who was very much enslaved to the ways of the world.

When I was about twenty years old, I sold drugs to an undercover law enforcement officer and, as a result, was convicted of a felony. During the punishment phase of my trial, God saw fit to bring a believer into my life. The person He chose was my cellmate. It just so happened that he was fasting.

New to the Lord and still ignorant about many aspects of the Bible, I asked him what the purpose of a fast was. He took the time to explain to me that during a fast, believers deny their material needs in order to devote more time to God and draw closer to Him. My exact response to him was, "Praise God, I need to do that." I followed in my cellmate's footsteps and spent time getting closer to the Lord, and He rewarded me for it. I was facing fifteen years to life, but God touched the heart of the judge and he instead sentenced me to only two years. I still had to pay for my transgressions, but a loving God bestowed mercy upon me for seeking Him in faith. Thank you, Jesus.

God took hold of my heart that day, and He has been a part of my life ever since. I have come to know a deep and abiding love for Him, and I find great comfort and strength through the study of His holy Word. Out of that love, I have put together this collection of devotionals so you may come to be blessed as truly as I have. It is my sincere hope and prayer that the words I have been led to share do just that.

May our Heavenly Father pour out His love and blessings upon you now and forever more.

Darrell Reynolds

¹Unless the LORD builds the house,
the builders labor in vain.
Unless the LORD watches over the city,
the guards stand watch in vain.

Psalm 127:1 NIV

⁶And without faith it is impossible to please God, because anyone who comes to him must believe that he exists and that he rewards those who earnestly seek him.

Hebrews 11:6 NIV

WEEK ONE

Actions

¹The beginning of the good news about Jesus the Messiah, the Son of God, ²as it is written in Isaiah the prophet:

> *'I will send my messenger ahead of you,*
> *who will prepare your way.'*

Mark 1:1-2 NIV

We often do things without considering what the consequence of our actions may be. As God's people, however, we should always choose which actions we will take based on what is right in the eyes of the Lord. Jesus actions proved who He was and where He was from. Part of His purpose was to serve as our example, to go before us and prepare the way we are meant to walk. Our actions, then, should do the same for other followers of the cross.

Wednesday

Hold Up Under Pressure

12Fight the good fight of the faith. Take hold of the eternal life to which you were called when you made your good confession in the presence of many witnesses.

1 Timothy 6:12 NIV

We must not give up when pressure mounts during our walk with Jesus Christ. As Paul urged Timothy, we must instead continue to "fight the good fight of the faith," always remembering that Jesus is with us each step of the way. When going through trials and tribulations, we must maintain our faith and trust in the Word because, if truth be told, the difficulties we face only come into our lives to make us stronger and to grow us in the love of our God.

WEEK TWO

Sunday

Trust

³⁵So do not throw away your confidence; it will be richly rewarded.
Hebrews 10:35 NIV

Jesus told His disciples, "Do not let your hearts be troubled. You believe in God; believe also in me." (John 14:1 NIV) These words should bring us comfort because we *can* trust in both God and the Lord Jesus Christ, fully and absolutely, at all times. In fact, we must believe and know that trust itself comes from God. When we need someone we can trust one hundred percent, one hundred percent of the time, we must exercise our confidence in God. It *will* be richly rewarded, just as Scripture promises.

Wednesday

The Holy Spirit Is Our Teacher

⁶We do, however, speak a message of wisdom among the mature, but not the wisdom of this age or the rulers of this age, who are coming to nothing. ⁷No, we declare God's wisdom, a mystery that has been hidden and that God destined for our glory before time began. ⁸None of the rulers of this age understood it, for if they had, they would not have crucified the Lord of glory. ⁹However, as it is written:

> *'What no eye has seen,*
> *what no ear has heard,*
> *and what no human mind has conceived'—*
> > *the things God has prepared for those who love him—*
> > *¹⁰these are the things God has revealed to us by his Spirit.*

1 Corinthians 2:6-10 NIV

The Word of God never says that man will teach anything of lasting value or importance. It *does* say, however, that the Holy Spirit will teach us and lead us in all truth. God may very well use other men or women to reveal His truths to us, but these revelations will only be made through the power of His Spirit. What He does reveal, we should receive with reverence (Deuteronomy 4:10), for it will be greater than anything we could ever imagine.

WEEK THREE

Sunday

Keep That Sword Ready

²He made my mouth like a sharpened sword,
in the shadow of his hand he hid me;
he made me into a polished arrow
and concealed me in his quiver.

Isaiah 49:2 NIV

We are to follow in the spiritual footsteps of our Lord and Savior Jesus Christ, the subject of these verses. The Word of God exhorts us to praise the Lord for He "trains [our] hands for war, [our] fingers for battle" (Psalm 144:1 NIV). Just as Jesus took a stand against sin, so must we stand, from sunrise to nightfall, with sword drawn, ready to profess the Word of God and do the same.

Wednesday

Be Anxious About Nothing

⁶Do not be anxious about anything, but in every situation, by prayer and petition, with thanksgiving, present your requests to God.
Philippians 4:6 NIV

Being anxious weighs down our hearts (Proverb 12:25), and this weakens our ability to be of service to God. God's Word is always available to us so we can receive help when we need it most. We must allow it to teach us how we should approach troubles when they arise in our lives. Similarly, God's ears are always open to hear our prayers. When the things we may want to happen so badly in our lives do not turn out as we may have hoped, we can always lift our hearts to God and talk to Him about them. He *will* hear us and provide us with comfort.

WEEK FOUR

Sunday

Remain With The Word

⁸But what does it say? 'The word is near you; it is in your mouth and in your heart,' that is, the message concerning faith that we proclaim: ⁹If you declare with your mouth, 'Jesus is Lord,' and believe in your heart that God raised him from the dead, you will be saved. ¹⁰For it is with your heart that you believe and are justified, and it is with your mouth that you profess your faith and are saved.

Romans 10:8-10 NIV

We need the word of God. It is the only source of truth—honest to goodness, sincere truth—mankind has been given. It will never lead us astray, so we should take heed of what it instructs us to do—especially in matters of faith. If we sincerely believe in the Lord Jesus Christ, we must profess this belief with the utmost confidence. Some of the people we associate with may have nothing more to do with us as a result, but no matter what happens, God will never leave us (Deuteronomy 31:8). He is the greatest person in all of creation, and He has chosen to reveal Himself to us through His Word. If we remain with the Word of God, by extension, we will also stay with God Himself.

Wednesday

Write Your Vision

¹I will stand at my watch
and station myself on the ramparts;
I will look to see what he will say to me,
and what answer I am to give to this complaint...
²Then the LORD replied:
'Write down the revelation
and make it plain on tablets
so that a herald may run with it.
For the revelation awaits an appointed time;
it speaks of the end
and will not prove false.'

Habakkuk 2:1-2 NIV

Our God is indeed an awesome God. He is love, and He freely bestows every ounce of His love—and, therefore, Himself—onto us. In fact, He loves us so much that He wants us to prosper in everything we do for Him (Jeremiah 29:11). He has given us instructions on how to do so. We are write down the visions He gives us—the hopes, the dreams—so we can keep our end goals in sight and develop plans to achieve them. If these things are really God-sent inspirations, if they are truly in accordance with His will, He *will* make them happen. The Word, will, and promises of God are that certain.

WEEK FIVE

Sunday

The Great Physician

¹Some time later, Jesus went up to Jerusalem for one of the Jewish festivals. ²Now there is in Jerusalem near the Sheep Gate a pool, which in Aramaic is called Bethesda and which is surrounded by five covered colonnades. ³Here a great number of disabled people used to lie—the blind, the lame, the paralyzed—and they waited for the moving of the waters. ⁴From time to time an angel of the Lord would come down and stir up the waters. The first one into the pool after each such disturbance would be cured of whatever disease they had. ⁵One who was there had been an invalid for thirty-eight years. ⁶When Jesus saw him lying there and learned that he had been in this condition for a long time, he asked him, 'Do you want to get well?'

⁷'Sir,' the invalid replied, 'I have no one to help me into the pool when the water is stirred. While I am trying to get in, someone else goes down ahead of me.'

⁸Then Jesus said to him, 'Get up! Pick up your mat and walk.' ⁹At once the man was cured; he picked up his mat and walked.

John 5:1-9 NIV

Truly, we can thank God for being the great I AM. Just as truly, we can thank Jesus for being the great Physician. When we are troubled or ill, we can rely on doctors, scientists, and even fortune tellers if we wish, but no one can ever heal us—ever *truly* heal us—except Jesus. He is the only One who can ever really take care of us, the only one who can lift us beyond even the most difficult or painful situation. All we need to do is call on Him.

Wednesday

Avoid Negative Talk

²⁰He went on: 'What comes out of a person is what defiles them. ²¹For it is from within, out of a person's heart, that evil thoughts come— sexual immorality, theft, murder, ²²adultery, greed, malice, deceit, lewdness, envy, slander, arrogance and folly. ²³All these evils come from inside and defile a person.'

Mark 7:20-23 NIV

When we become believers, we also become family to God Almighty. As sons and daughters of the Lord, we have to walk accordingly. In order to do this, we must change not only how we think and act, but also how we talk. We must strive to avoid speaking negatively and instead let our words be like rays of light in an otherwise dark world. Just as importantly, as much as it is possible, we must not allow negative words to enter our ears and, by extension, our hearts. If we do, we will soon be no different than those still enslaved to the ways of the world. We are to be ministers of the Word. Let us, therefore, make every effort to share and show love in all we do and say wherever we may go.

WEEK SIX

Sunday

Do Everything In His Name

[17]And whatever you do, whether in word or deed, do it all in the name of the Lord Jesus, giving thanks to God the Father through him.
Colossians 3:17 NIV

Those who belong to the world live only to exalt mankind. When we begin walking with Jesus Christ, however, we come to understand that everything we say and do must instead be for Him and for His glory. If we acknowledge that, if we honestly live our lives grounded in this belief, then all our words and deeds truly can be offered in His perfect name.

Wednesday

Choices

⁶When the woman saw that the fruit of the tree was good for food and pleasing to the eye, and also desirable for gaining wisdom, she took some and ate it. She also gave some to her husband, who was with her, and he ate it. ⁷Then the eyes of both of them were opened, and they realized they were naked; so they sewed fig leaves together and made coverings for themselves.

⁸Then the man and his wife heard the sound of the LORD GOD AS HE WAS WALKING IN THE GARDEN IN THE COOL OF THE DAY, AND THEY HID FROM THE LORD GOD AMONG THE TREES OF THE GARDEN.

Genesis 3:6-8 NIV

We serve the God of heaven and earth, and He has given us the free will to make choices in life. Whether they are good or bad choices depends upon whose desires we seek to fulfill—our own or the Lord's. Adam and Eve chose to act according to their own wishes rather than heed the will of God, and only disaster followed (Genesis 3:14-19). The decision to either serve ourselves or serve the Lord exists for us today, just as it did for Adam and Eve all those years ago. We, too, can rebel against God, or we can live to serve Him. The choice is ours.

WEEK SEVEN

Sunday

Follow The Leader

[18] And he is the head of the body, the church; he is the beginning and the firstborn from among the dead, so that in everything he might have the supremacy.

Colossians 1:18 NIV

Have you ever wanted to know why you were born when you were, what the purpose of your life may be, or what you were put on this earth to achieve? Although people seek the answers to questions like these in many places, there is only one Person who can actually lay them to rest—Jesus. He is the Head of all God's churches on earth, the Head of the body of believers, and the Head of our individual bodies as well. Born without sin, raised from the dead, and soon to return in glory—now, that is a leader we should *all* be following, even into eternity.

Wednesday

Exercise Your Patience

²²We know that the whole creation has been groaning as in the pains of childbirth right up to the present time. ²³Not only so, but we ourselves, who have the firstfruits of the Spirit, groan inwardly as we wait eagerly for our adoption to sonship, the redemption of our bodies. ²⁴For in this hope we were saved. But hope that is seen is no hope at all. Who hopes for what they already have? ²⁵But if we hope for what we do not yet have, we wait for it patiently.

Romans 8:22-25 NIV

In this life, we are going to face circumstances that will test our patience on a daily basis. These experiences will not be easy to endure, but we must if we are going to grow to be like Christ. Remember, we fail to serve God in the manner He deserves and, therefore, try His patience on a daily basis as well. Still, He does not abandon us (Hebrews 13:5). He has demonstrated His own patience toward us by sending His Son to pave the way to salvation, despite our sinful ways (John 3:16, Romans 5:8). We should all remember that the next time we feel the urge to be impatient ourselves.

WEEK EIGHT

Sunday

You Have Access To God

¹⁴Therefore, since we have a great high priest who has ascended into heaven, Jesus the Son of God, let us hold firmly to the faith we profess. ¹⁵For we do not have a high priest who is unable to empathize with our weaknesses, but we have one who has been tempted in every way, just as we are—yet he did not sin. ¹⁶Let us then approach God's throne of grace with confidence, so that we may receive mercy and find grace to help us in our time of need.

Hebrews 4:14-16 NIV

The Bible clearly expresses God's desire for us to experience fellowship with Him (John 17:23, 1 John 1:3). What is so wonderful about this is that we can take part is such fellowship *at all times*. Whether we are on the mountaintop or in the valley makes no difference—nothing can ever separate us from Him (Romans 8:35-39). Because of this, we can always approach Him with confidence. That is the beauty of our faith; whenever we need God, He is already right there with us, ready and able to do what man cannot (Psalm 145:18).

Wednesday

Don't Count On Tomorrow

¹Do not boast about tomorrow,
for you do not know what a day may bring.
Proverb 27:1 NIV

Each day of our lives has been given to us so we can bring glory to God That being true, we must not take even a single one of them for granted. We should instead cherish each day and live it as Jesus did, working in the field doing God's work. No one is promised tomorrow, and each day has work enough to tend to (Matthew 6:34). Let us, therefore, do everything we can for God in the time we have been allotted today.

WEEK NINE

Sunday

Man Has Been Given Dominion

26 Then God said, 'Let us make mankind in our image, in our likeness, so that they may rule over the fish in the sea and the birds in the sky, over the livestock and all the wild animals, and over all the creatures that move along the ground.'

Genesis 1:26 NIV

Our God is a sovereign God—the Ruler of all creation—yet He has chosen to entrust mankind with stewardship of the earth. This was a specific part of God's master plan. The first man and woman He created He made to be partners in this endeavor (Genesis 2:18). The fact that God fashioned these people—and, by extension, all of their descendants—in His own image is a significant one. He intended for mankind to rule over the earth, to have dominion over all living things, but to do so as He would—with Godly wisdom. Such wisdom can only be found in His Word and related through consistent communion with Him. Let us, therefore, seek this wisdom daily so that we can be faithful stewards of His creation.

Wednesday

From The Old You To The New You

17 Therefore, if anyone is in Christ, the new creation has come: The old has gone, the new is here!

2 Corinthians 5:17 NIV

When we surrender our lives to God, we cannot do so halfheartedly. Our devotion to the Lord must be absolute. Though we will stumble in our daily walks with God, our intention must be to totally abandon our old ways of living and instead embrace His. By and through the power of His Son, Jesus Christ, we become "new creations" dedicated to giving God. This does not mean our lives will suddenly become trouble-free, but rather that we will be able to rejoice in our sufferings when they arise (Romans 5:3-5), as well as find the strength we need to endure them without fear and without fail (Philippians 4:13).

WEEK TEN

Sunday

Avoid Spiritual Laziness

¹¹Never be lacking in zeal, but keep your spiritual fervor, serving the Lord.

Romans 12:11 NIV

"The LORD is a warrior…" (Exodus 15:3 NIV). We must also be warriors if we are going to be of useful service to Him. Lazy people are full of excuses and will say anything to avoid taking action (Proverb 22:13; 26:13). Warriors of God, however, are willing to fight the darkness in the world with the power of His Word, ready and eager to do so whenever He commands. Spiritual laziness can only lead to spiritual poverty; if we maintain our spiritual fervor, however, we will never want for blessing (Proverb 10:4).

Wednesday

Seek Generosity Over Greed

35 When they had crucified him, they divided up his clothes by casting lots. 36 And sitting down, they kept watch over him there. 37 Above his head they placed the written charge against him: THIS IS JESUS, THE KING OF THE JEWS.

Matthew 27:35-37 NIV

The more we own, the more distracted we can become. Just like the Roman soldiers who cast lots for Jesus' clothing, we can become so absorbed with gaining wealth and material possessions that we miss feeling the presence of God even when He is right there in our midst. Unlike the value system of the world, the worth of a Christian's life is not measured by the abundance of "stuff" a person may possess, but by the abundance of love he or she demonstrates to others. Because our possessions are truly only blessings from the Lord, we should never be afraid to bless others through them as well. As we have freely received, so should we freely give (Matthew 10:8).

WEEK ELEVEN

Sunday

By Faith

⁶And without faith it is impossible to please God, because anyone who comes to him must believe that he exists and that he rewards those who earnestly seek him.

Hebrews 11:6 NIV

We live our daily lives in the natural world. Many of the things we witness and experience we accept without a second thought; we see them and believe in what we saw. Some of these things are very dark, however, and without God they could become so discouraging as to be overwhelming. That is one of the many reasons we need God. He *can* and *will* carry us through even the darkest points of our lives if only we will seek Him in faith and believe in the depth of His love for us. It is impossible to please Him any other way.

Wednesday

The Unquenchable Fire Of God

29'Is not my word like fire,' declares the LORD, 'and like a hammer that breaks a rock in pieces?'

Jeremiah 23:29 NIV

God means what He says when He speaks. Scripture tells us that the Word of God will not return void but will instead accomplish the purpose for which He has determined it (Isaiah 55:11). Like a fire moving through a forest, the Word of God will continue to spread leaving change in its wake. With enough effort, man can quench a fire, but He cannot stop the power of the Lord. As believers, we have been called to preach His Word to every creature. If we have not already begun to do so, we should begin immediately.

WEEK TWELVE

Sunday

Growing Spiritually

¹⁵My eyes are ever on the LORD,
for only he will release my feet from the snare.

Psalm 25:15 NIV

If we are going to grow spiritually, one of the rules we must follow is that we must never take our eyes off the Lord. The moment we do so, the moment we instead cast a glance to the circumstances swirling around us, we begin to sink (Matthew 14:28-31). We must not, therefore, allow the trials or challenges we may face in this life deter us from drawing closer to God. In fact, they should do just the opposite—they should push us *closer* to Him. The enemy cannot stop our spiritual growth. The Lord will shelter us and give us increase if only we will maintain focus on Him and walk with boldness, full of the light of His love.

Wednesday

Obey God Immediately

*[60]I will hasten and not delay,
to obey your commands.*

Psalm 119:60 NIV

No matter what God asks of us, He expects an immediate response. It may not be something we can accomplish the moment we hear His voice, but it *is* something we can respond to and begin preparing for right that second. Lot delayed when the Lord sent angels to carry His command, and the results were disastrous (Genesis 19:1-29). By comparison, Noah took immediate action and he was blessed (Genesis 6:9-9:3). The words of God are "now words." He speaks because He wants something done and preparation for such must begin immediately. When God spoke the world into existence, everything lined up right then and there as He commanded. We, too, are part of God's creation. We should align ourselves with His commands the instant we hear them as well.

WEEK THIRTEEN

Sunday

Sheep And Goats

³All the nations will be gathered before him, and he will separate the people one from another as a shepherd separates the sheep from the goats.

Matthew 25:32 NIV

If we pay even slight attention to the news today, it is very clear that not everyone who calls him- or herself a Christian is really as believer. In some cases, entire churches have turned away from truth and started preaching messages full of misleading information (2 Timothy 4:3-4). There shall come a time, however, when the Lord will separate charlatans from His own chosen people. This will occur on the Judgment Day, at which time we will all be identified for what we really are and will be rewarded or punished accordingly. If we are truly the Lord's sheep, if He truly is our Shepherd, we must heed His voice and seek to accomplish what He commands in the time He has granted us to do so.

Wednesday

We Are Never Trapped

14In days to come, when your son asks you, 'What does this mean?' say to him, 'With a mighty hand the LORD BROUGHT US OUT OF EGYPT, OUT OF THE LAND OF SLAVERY.'

Exodus 13:14 NIV

When Moses led Israel out of slavery in Egypt, those who followed him experienced moments of doubt and fear when their circumstances became overwhelming. Had they only been justified.no mere man could have delivered them, trapped as they were with the sea on one side and the their enemy on the other. Moses,however,was following God; in truth,then,it was the lord who was setting them free. As such, they had no need to fear because nothing is beyond His power to overcome. Like Israel people, we have all felt trapped by our circumstances at some point in our lives. Also like the Israel people, we serve a God who can and will deliver us from our trials if we rely on Him to do so.God,the father; Jesus, the son; and the Godhead will always deliver us; we can never be trapped by anything if we place our faith in God.

WEEK FOURTEEN

Sunday

Trust In God Above Money

²⁴No one can serve two masters. Either you will hate the one and love the other, or you will be devoted to the one and despise the other. You cannot serve both God and money.

Matthew 6:24 NIV

Without question, God wants to bless us abundantly, but He also wants to be the center of our lives (Matthew 6:33). With the multitude of distractions vying for our attention in the world today, it is very easy to be swayed from our love for God. We can easily begin placing our focus on far less important things, things which can never sustain us for long—especially our wealth. While money itself is not evil, the love of money is (1 Timothy 6:10). We must not let our pursuit of wealth overtake our pursuit of the Lord. Jesus said, "It is written, 'Man shall not live by bread alone, but by every word that comes from the mouth of God'" (Matthew 4:4 NIV). Let us, then, seek God above all things, giving Him glory for whatever we may possess, for it is He who bestows all things upon us.

Wednesday

Give God A Tenth

22Be sure to set aside a tenth of all that your fields produce each year.
Deuteronomy 14:22 NIV

People never seem to be at a loss for words when it comes to money, especially when they are being asked to give some of it away. Even Christians fall victim to this. Some believe that tithing—setting aside for God a tenth of our income—is no longer required because it is not explicitly mentioned anywhere in the New Testament. Others believe it is only a suggestion and that they can actually give less. Still others believe they should only give if they have a say in how the money they part with is spent. The truth is that all we possess has been given to us by God (James 1:17); our wealth, therefore, is really not ours at all, but His. God commands us to tithe, to return to Him a tenth of what He has freely given to us. As in all other aspects of our lives, we would be wise to obey Him in this regard.

WEEK FIFTEEN

Sunday

God's Plans Are Greater Than Your Own

[11] *'For I know the plans I have for you,' declares the* LORD, *'PLANS TO PROSPER YOU AND NOT TO HARM YOU, PLANS TO GIVE YOU HOPE AND A FUTURE.'*

Jeremiah 29:11 NIV

We all make plans. Every single one of us has goals he or she has set, a vision of how his or her life will hopefully turn out. We begin to form such things as children with our dreams of being doctors, policemen or policewomen, even President of the United States. There is no harm in doing this. Positive thinking, after all, usually brings about positive results. But God has plans for us as well. That is actually an amazing thing to consider because the plans of God are always more detailed and more rewarding than any we could ever make for ourselves. We should, therefore, take heed to what God's plans for our lives may be. We should likewise allow His plans to take precedence over our own. What we will is not important; what the Lord wills is (Luke 22:42).

Wednesday

Jesus Is Speaking…Are You Listening?

[7]Surely the Sovereign LORD does nothing without revealing his plan to his servants the prophets.

Amos 3:7 NIV

When God speaks to us, it is safe to assume that He is doing so because He has something very important to say. It is His will that we listen to Him and obey whatever He may command us to do. Just as He has a plan for our lives, so, too, does God have a plan for the entire world. He has chosen to allow His people to be a part of that plan. Whatever God reveals to us, therefore, we must join with Him to bring to pass. As believers, it is our responsibility to bring Him glory in all things. Trusting in Him, in His Word, and in His plans—living in the Spirit while we are granted time on this earth—will do just that.

WEEK SIXTEEN

Sunday

God's Blessings Always Bring A Positive Return

¹⁷Every good and perfect gift is from above, coming down from the Father of the heavenly lights, who does not change like shifting shadows.

James 1:17 NIV

A number of things happen in our lives each and every day—some of them are planned or expected; others most definitely are not. Even when things are planned, however, they do not necessarily turn out as we hope they will. That is just the way of the world. With so much chaos and uncertainty present in society today, it is impossible to trust in the fact that we will always receive a good return for our labors. With God, however, this is not the case. Unlike the ever-changing nature of the world, God is constant—"the same yesterday and today and forever" (Hebrews 13:8 NIV). Without fail, what He chooses to bestow upon us will be good every time.

Wednesday

God Gave You A Message For The World

36But I tell you that everyone will have to give account on the day of judgment for every empty word they have spoken.

Matthew 12:36 NIV

Every word we speak is important, but many people either waste them bickering and trying to win pointless arguments or discussing the value of issues that quickly pass away. Relatively few judge their words carefully enough to ensure that they convey something of lasting, eternal value. God gave us His one and only Son so we could have life (John 3:16). He did not do this so we could squander our lives engaging in foolish talk, however. He gave us life so we could share the Good News of His Word. God has given us a message to share with the rest of the world. If we are not already doing so, we should change that immediately. Empty words cannot change lives; words filled with the power of God, however, can.

WEEK SEVENTEEN

Sunday

God Is Good

¹⁸'Why do you call me good?' Jesus answered. 'No one is good—except God alone.'

Mark 10:18 NIV

Everything God has made is good (Genesis 1:31). God Himself is the essence of goodness; there is nothing dark or evil either about Him or within Him (1 John 1:5). The same thing cannot be said of us. Even though we may see people doing good things in the world, they are still touched by sin. Even the most righteous person still falls short when compared to the absolute perfection and purity of the Lord. When the Jewish people saw Jesus, they witnessed the perfection of God's character firsthand. They could rightly call Him good because He walked among them as God in the flesh. You and I are not good in an of ourselves, but as we live for the Lord and follow the commands set forth in His Word to love others as He loves us, we will reflect God's goodness and, in turn, bring Him glory.

Wednesday

God's Wisdom

> [5]*Trust in the* L*ORD* *with all your heart*
> *and lean not on your own understanding;*
> [6]*in all your ways submit to him,*
> *and he will make your paths straight.*

Proverb 3:5-6 NIV

When God made you and I, He knew we would face situations when we would need His wisdom. Time and time again we encounter people or circumstances we cannot handle on our own. This is not an accident; it is all according God's design. Whatever challenge, hardship, or tragedy we may face, the thing we must remember is that God wants us to seek Him so He can carry us through. God already has the answer. If we will call on Him in faith, relying on Him and trusting in Him with all our hearts, He will provide us with the wisdom we need to respond accordingly.

WEEK EIGHTEEN

Sunday

Make Your Declarations With The Power Of God

28What you decide on will be done,
and light will shine on your way.
Job 22:28 NIV

God has created us in His likeness; He expects us to speak and act in ways that will bring Him glory. As we allow the blood of His Son to cover us, as we allow His Spirit to not only dwell within us but also direct our course, as we live in accord with His Word, He will work through us to make things happen in the spiritual realm. As long as it is in the will of God and in accordance with His plans, what we declare in the name of Jesus will bring blessings to others and also advance the Kingdom of God. Neither man nor Satan will be able to stand against us.

Wednesday

The Word Of God

¹In the beginning was the Word, and the Word was with God, and the Word was God. ²He was with God in the beginning. ³Through him all things were made; without him nothing was made that has been made. ⁴In him was life, and that life was the light of all mankind. ⁵The light shines in the darkness, and the darkness has not overcome it.'

John 1:1-5 NIV

Without the Word of God, mankind would be in a hopeless position. When we look at the events transpiring in the world today, things look bleak enough. Can you imagine where we would be if the light of God did not exist? Thank God—literally—that His Word became flesh and came to earth in the form of Jesus to save mankind from sin. God is a God of second chances; it is up to us to accept them when they are offered. When we stray from God, we can always find Him again through His Word. It was with Him from the beginning; it is with us as well—today and forever.

WEEK NINETEEN

Sunday

As You Listen To The Birds, Listen To Me

> *⁷But ask the animals, and they will teach you,*
> *or the birds in the sky, and they will tell you;*
> *⁸or speak to the earth, and it will teach you,*
> *or let the fish in the sea inform you.*
> *⁹Which of all these does not know*
> *that the hand of the LORD HAS DONE THIS?*
> *¹⁰In his hand is the life of every creature*
> *and the breath of all mankind.*
>
> **Job 12:7-10 NIV**

It is an understatement to say that God has done a lot for us. What is more, everything He has done has been on His own initiative. He did not need to be asked or otherwise prompted. It is His will, it is His very nature, to love us—period. Everything He has done for us has been borne from this love. When He comes to us wanting to speak to us and lead us to places where He can bless us, the very least we can do is listen. If we do, we will find His voice even more beautiful than those of the birds we love so much.

Wednesday

The One Path To Heaven

⁵Thomas said to him, 'Lord, we don't know where you are going, so how can we know the way?'

⁶Jesus answered, 'I am the way and the truth and the life. No one comes to the Father except through me. ⁷If you really know me, you will know my Father as well. From now on, you do know him and have seen him.'

John 14:5-7 NIV

There are many religions being practiced in the world today. Many of them are gaining popularity because they preach that we can make it into Heaven—or whatever name they use to label their equivalent of such—by being good or by performing certain actions or by following certain rules. This is a lie, of course, one being carried into the world by the "prince of the air" himself (Ephesians 2:2). Of all the major world religions, only Christianity says that we are powerless to reach Heaven through our own efforts. Mankind would never create a religion that would limit its power to do anything, so this only confirms the divine origin of our faith. Trust in God and trust in the truth revealed in His Word. There is only one way to enter an eternity shared with God, and that way is through His Son, Jesus Christ.

WEEK TWENTY

Sunday

Let God Plan Your Steps

⁹In their hearts humans plan their course,
but the LORD establishes their steps.

Proverb 16:9 NIV

Although we make decisions in life, we do not always follow through with them. We allow things to distract us from our goals, and sometimes we abandon them altogether as a result. When it comes to the Lord and His plans, however, the path we must follow is a straight one. If God has a purpose for us, He will not allow us to deviate from it. He will guide our choices and, through them, lead us where He desires us to go.

Wednesday

Overcome The World

[33]I have told you these things, so that in me you may have peace. In this world you will have trouble. But take heart! I have overcome the world.

John 16:33 NIV

When horrible things take place in the world, some people question how a loving God could allow them to happen. Whenever something tragic occurs, these people often say, "If God *really* loved the world, He would have stopped this from happening." As believers, we know that God sits on the throne of Heaven with all the power of the universe at His command. We also know, however, that we were all born into a sinful world, and sin will continue to bring heartache and loss until Jesus returns to set all things right once again. Christians, too, are saddened when bad things happen, but because we live by faith, we can stand on the Word of God and walk with Jesus, trusting in the truth that no lasting harm will befall us because God will never allow us to endure more than we can bear (1 Corinthians 10:13).

WEEK TWENTY-ONE

Sunday

The Spring Of Living Water

⁶He said to me: 'It is done. I am the Alpha and the Omega, the Beginning and the End. To the thirsty I will give water without cost from the spring of the water of life.'

Revelation 21:6 NIV

Once we truly taste the love of Jesus Christ, nothing else in this world will ever be able to satisfy us. Jesus died upon the cross for our sins, even while we were still His enemies (Romans 5:8). That is how much He loves us. What is more, He conquered the grave by raising Himself from the dead and, in doing so, became a "spring of the water of life" for those who believe so they could enjoy eternal life with Him (John 4:14). He gives us His love freely; everything He has done for us He has done with no request for payment other than to love Him in return. No gift could ever be greater than that.

Wednesday

With Jesus You Can Do The Impossible

23 'If you can?' said Jesus. 'Everything is possible for one who believes.'
Mark 9:23 NIV

Every one of us has tried to do something in life but failed in his or her efforts to do so. Simply put, there are things in this world that we cannot make happen through our own strength. The good news is that God sent His Son to make these impossible things possible. With even the smallest amount of faith in the person and power of Jesus Christ, we can do *all* things (Matthew 17:20; 19:26). If only we will believe this truth and walk in it daily, God will do great things in and through our lives.

WEEK TWENTY-TWO

Sunday

Rewind Your Mind

> [18] *Who is a God like you,*
>   *who pardons sin and forgives the transgression*
> *of the remnant of his inheritance?*
>   *You do not stay angry forever*
> *but delight to show mercy.*
>
> **Micah 7:18 NIV**

Unfortunately, our lives are not like videos we have recorded. We cannot just press rewind and start over when things go wrong, and we cannot fast forward when something we do not like happens in our lives. Instead, we have to go through both the good and bad times as they come, living with the decisions we make as we go. Our God, however, is a merciful God, and He has given us His Word to guide our steps. Some say God has given us the Bible to be "**B**asic **I**nstructions **B**efore **L**eaving **E**arth." This may be true, but it is also so much more. God has had His hands on each one of us from the beginning, and He will use His Word to teach us and bless us if we will seek to know Him through it. Scripture will show us the errors of our sinful thinking and enable us to shift its focus from the world back to God where it belongs.

Wednesday

Walk With Power

¹One day Peter and John were going up to the temple at the time of prayer—at three in the afternoon. ²Now a man who was lame from birth was being carried to the temple gate called Beautiful, where he was put every day to beg from those going into the temple courts. ³When he saw Peter and John about to enter, he asked them for money. ⁴Peter looked straight at him, as did John. Then Peter said, 'Look at us!' ⁵So the man gave them his attention, expecting to get something from them.

⁶Then Peter said, 'Silver or gold I do not have, but what I do have I give you. In the name of Jesus Christ of Nazareth, walk.' ⁷Taking him by the right hand, he helped him up, and instantly the man's feet and ankles became strong. ⁸He jumped to his feet and began to walk.

Acts 3:1-7 NIV

If we want to walk with power, we have to first walk with Christ. Satan tries to convince us that there are other paths that will lead us to the same end—through attainment of wealth, possessions, popularity, or esteem, for example. The truth is that God has established a law that we must follow, a law that was exemplified in the perfect life of Jesus. It is life lived in accordance with this law and guided by the Holy Spirit that brings true power. God states in His word that, "…my people are destroyed for lack of knowledge" (Hosea 4:6 NIV). If we seek to do things based on our own understanding, we will eventually find our lives in ruin. The knowledge we need to prosper can only be found in Scripture. We should, therefore, consult and study it daily.

WEEK TWENTY-THREE

Sunday

Your Heavenly Account

¹⁹Do not store up for yourselves treasures on earth, where moths and vermin destroy, and where thieves break in and steal. ²⁰But store up for yourselves treasures in heaven, where moths and vermin do not destroy, and where thieves do not break in and steal. ²¹For where your treasure is, there your heart will be also.

Matthew 6:19-21 NIV

For as long as we live upon the earth, we will be tempted to obtain material wealth in some form or fashion. Some would say that the more wealth we possess, the more worthy we are—that the more we are able to leave behind, the more successfully we have lived our lives. The sad truth, however, is that no matter how much we obtain throughout our lives, none of us can take even a single penny with us when we depart the earth. Instead of striving to accumulate material goods, therefore, we should instead seek to add to the heavenly account each of us has with God. We can do this by loving others as He does and by acting on this love through our service to others. As God has given unto us, so should we cheerfully give unto others in return (2 Corinthians 9:7).

Wednesday

Don't Play The Fool

⁷The fear of the LORD is the beginning of knowledge,
but fools despise wisdom and instruction.

Proverb 1:7 NIV

According to the Word of God, to be a fool is to know that "right" teaching exists, but to pursue "wrong" teaching nonetheless. Some people have to learn the hard way, but those who are wise will heed the counsel of others so they do not make similar mistakes. As believers, we should all seek to be wise and allow God to direct us through the instruction, rebuke, correction, and training He can provide us though His Word (2 Timothy 3:16).

WEEK TWENTY-FOUR

Sunday

Accept Others Just As They Are

⁵May the God who gives endurance and encouragement give you the same attitude of mind toward each other that Christ Jesus had, ⁶so that with one mind and one voice you may glorify the God and Father of our Lord Jesus Christ.

⁷Accept one another, then, just as Christ accepted you, in order to bring praise to God.

Romans 15:5-7 NIV

It is easy to pass judgment on others because of where they were raised or where they went to school, how they dress or speak, or even what beliefs they hold. It is also easy to seek separation from those we consider to be less that ourselves once such judgments are rendered. As children of God, however, we should recognize that each and every person on this earth has been born into sin and will remain lost to its evil ways unless we accept the saving grace of Christ, the Lord. Tainted in this manner as we all are, none of us has ground to judge anyone else. Just as Jesus accepts us exactly as we are when we come to Him, so must we accept those around us. Our job is not to condemn, but to be vessels which God can use to carry His message to the world. This can only be accomplished through loving acceptance of the lost.

Wednesday

Glorify God In All You Do

*³¹So whether you eat or drink or whatever
you do, do it all for the glory of God.*
1 Corinthians 10:31 NIV

No matter what may come our way, because He has promised never to leave our side and never to forsake us (Deuteronomy 31:6) we can always be certain that the Lord is with us. Because God is infinitely greater than anything we could ever face, those who live by faith can also live with confidence. If we are willing to truly dedicate our lives to God, His very nature will be reflected in our character and every action we take will bring Him greater glory.

WEEK TWENTY-FIVE

Sunday

Put On The Armor Of God

[11] Put on the full armor of God, so that you can take your stand against the devil's schemes. [12] For our struggle is not against flesh and blood, but against the rulers, against the authorities, against the powers of this dark world and against the spiritual forces of evil in the heavenly realms. [13] Therefore put on the full armor of God, so that when the day of evil comes, you may be able to stand your ground, and after you have done everything, to stand. [14] Stand firm then, with the belt of truth buckled around your waist, with the breastplate of righteousness in place, [15] and with your feet fitted with the readiness that comes from the gospel of peace. [16] In addition to all this, take up the shield of faith, with which you can extinguish all the flaming arrows of the evil one. [17] Take the helmet of salvation and the sword of the Spirit, which is the word of God.

Ephesians 6:11-17 NIV

The armor of God covers us from head to toe. Whenever we wear it, not only are we fully protected from whatever the enemy may attempt to bring against us, but we are also fully prepared to be of service to God in the advancement of His kingdom. Certainly we will face trials in our lives, and we may very well experience momentary setbacks. But as long as we remain covered by the armor God provides us, nothing will ever conquer us. After facing whatever has come our way, we will still be able to stand and press on for Him.

Wednesday

A Spiritual Billiard Game

*¹⁶So I say, walk by the Spirit, and you will
not gratify the desires of the flesh.*

Galatians 5:16 NIV

In some ways, the Christian life is like a game of billiards. The
Holy Spirit is the cue; He is responsible for determining the path
we must follow in order to reach our destination and He is the
catalyst for setting in motion the events that will bring us to that
point. Believers are the cue ball; we are responsible for following
the course laid out for us, touching as many other lives as possible
along the way and directing them along the same route. We
cannot allow worldly temptations to impede our progress or alter
our course or others will suffer as a result. This is not a game we
can play casually; it is one we must win. As we follow the guidance
of the Spirit, we will.

WEEK TWENTY-SIX

Sunday

Do Not Delay...Act

28Do not say to your neighbor,
'Come back tomorrow and I'll give it to you'—
when you already have it with you.

Proverb 3:28 NIV

Many people simply "go through the motions" in their lives. Days pass and each month they simply turn another page on their calendars. These are the people who say that they are going to "get things right" in their lives once work settles down, once all of their bills are paid, or once their kids are grown, but never actually get around to doing anything at all. No one is promised tomorrow (Proverb 27:1). For this reason, we should immediately take action when Jesus calls upon us to do so. Whether He is calling out to us regarding our need for salvation or seeking to use us in the service of His kingdom, makes no difference. Procrastination will only bring about complacency, and if we become complacent with the ways of this world, we will never be able to escape them.

Wednesday

You Cannot Make It Without Jesus

⁴Even to your old age and gray hairs
I am he, I am he who will sustain you.
I have made you and I will carry you;
I will sustain you and I will rescue you.

Isaiah 46:4 NIV

Only fools do not believe in God (Psalm 14:1). Not only are they fools because they doubt His existence, but also because they honestly believe they can survive without His care and guidance to carry them through each day. They live however they want to—and some even find happiness for a time—but ultimately all of these people still have voids in their lives only God can fill. One day, every knee shall bow before Jesus and every tongue will confess He is Lord (Philippians 2:10-11). Those of us who are wise enough to do these things while we walk this earth are promised strength enough to weather any storm. Only a true fool would refuse that.

WEEK TWENTY-SEVEN

Sunday

Be A Light Others Can Follow

¹⁴You are the light of the world. A town built on a hill cannot be hidden. ¹⁵Neither do people light a lamp and put it under a bowl. Instead they put it on its stand, and it gives light to everyone in the house. ¹⁶In the same way, let your light shine before others, that they may see your good deeds and glorify your Father in heaven.

Matthew 5:14-16 NIV

Jesus is the Light of the world (John 8:12). This was true when He physically walked upon the earth, and it is still true today. God, the Father, gave Him the wisdom He needed to live in perfect harmony with His Word. As His disciples, we are meant to reflect the light of Jesus to others by living through the power of His Spirit. More importantly, we are to seek out opportunities to do this instead of run from them. Our light—the Light of Jesus—is meant to be shared, never hidden.

Wednesday

God Will Heal Your Wounds

> ^{1}*Praise the* LORD*, my soul;*
> *all my inmost being, praise his holy name.*
> ^{2}*Praise the* LORD*, my soul,*
> *and forget not all his benefits—*
> ^{3}*who forgives all your sins*
> *and heals all your diseases,*
> ^{4}*who redeems your life from the pit*
> *and crowns you with love and compassion,*
> ^{5}*who satisfies your desires with good things*
> *so that your youth is renewed like the eagle's.*
> **Psalm 103:1-5 NIV**

When those in the world doubt the Word of God and say it is full of lies, that is only proof of their own ignorance. The Word of God is not only true, but also the revelation of Truth in the person of Jesus Christ. Throughout the Old Testament, God promises healing to those who live by faith in Him; throughout the New Testament, Jesus delivers healing to those who believe His words are true. Healing, deliverance, salvation—all gifts revealed in the Bible and bestowed upon those who sought after God with all their heart, soul, and strength—are still evident and available in the world today. We can claim them in exactly the same way those who came before us did—by faith.

WEEK TWENTY-EIGHT

Sunday

Jesus, Your Lord

²¹Not everyone who says to me, 'Lord, Lord,' will enter the kingdom of heaven, but only the one who does the will of my Father who is in heaven. ²²Many will say to me on that day, 'Lord, Lord, did we not prophesy in your name and in your name drive out demons and in your name perform many miracles?' ²³Then I will tell them plainly, 'I never knew you. Away from me, you evildoers!'

Matthew 7:21-23 NIV

The Lord is a Tower believers can run to in order to find safety when challenges arise in their lives (Proverb 18:10). He is a source of hope, strength, joy, and forgiveness for those who earnestly seek Him. Some people, however, call upon the Lord only when they need something. They read the Bible or go to church because they believe they can somehow earn God's blessings if they obey Him long enough to get what they want. God, of course, is all–knowing. These individuals cannot hide their motives from Him. People who try to use God like this are only fooling themselves. There will come a time when everyone will meet the Lord face to face. Those who lived to please Him, He will call His children. The names of those who lived only for themselves, however, He will not even know.

Wednesday

The Church

22 And God placed all things under his feet and appointed him to be head over everything for the church, 23 which is his body, the fullness of him who fills everything in every way.

Ephesians 1:22-23 NIV

Many people believe that the church is just a building they can visit to enjoy fellowship with other believers. Others believe it is a holy place where they can hear the voice of God and, through it, be restored in mind, body, and spirit. The church *is* these things, of course, but it is also much more. If we pay attention to Scripture, we see that the church is really composed of all those who believe in God and His Son, Jesus Christ. It is a body, an assembly of people who have sought to live blameless lives before the Lord. Every single believer—from the beginning of time until the end—is a part of this body, and Jesus is its Head. He will direct us and fill us, making us available to be used by God to expand His kingdom until Jesus' return.

WEEK TWENTY-NINE

Sunday

Discover Who You Are

12 Yet to all who did receive him, to those who believed in his name, he gave the right to become children of God—13 children born not of natural descent, nor of human decision or a husband's will, but born of God.

John 1:12-13 NIV

Throughout our lives, we spend a great deal of time and energy trying to identify who we are. Some people try to define themselves through their careers, others through how much wealth they can accumulate, and still others through the opinions of the people around them. Rather than define ourselves by worldly standards, however, we should instead seek to know who we are in God. We are all His children. He has created each one of us, as well as given us purpose in our lives. What is more, He has also given us gifts and talents to use in His service, as well as the power to daily overcome the temptations of our flesh so we may do so. Because of Him, we are more than conquerors (Romans 8:37); we are brothers and sisters of Christ Jesus and co-heirs to the Kingdom of Heaven (Romans 8:17).

Wednesday

You Hold The Key

18Truly I tell you, whatever you bind on earth will be bound in heaven, and whatever you loose on earth will be loosed in heaven.
Matthew 18:18 NIV

Believers have the opportunity to channel the very power of God in all they do. If truth be told, however, the key to unlocking this power rests in our speech. The words of believers have the power to make a difference in the world around them. We should, therefore, take great care to ensure that our words are spoken only to encourage others and build them up (Ephesians 4:29). If we see friends, family members, or even our enemies struggling with sin—or if we, ourselves, are being attacked by the enemy—we can repel these attacks through the Word of God. God is willing to unleash all the power of Heaven to aid us in our efforts. All we need to do is open our mouths and confidently speak in the name and power of Jesus Christ.

WEEK THIRTY

Sunday

Safe In The Hands Of God

29My Father, who has given them to me, is greater than all; no one can snatch them out of my Father's hand.

John 10:29 NIV

The life of a believer is a daily struggle between good and evil. Despite the fact that we have the very Spirit of God dwelling within us, we are also flesh-and-blood creatures who sometimes do what we know we should not (Romans 7:9). The devil would like nothing more than to pull us down and see us fail. He wants to take us as his own. Praise be to God that He is greater than the enemy and, as such, can and will keep us safe. Because God is our strength and our shield, neither the devil nor any demon in hell can stop us. We belong to God and God alone.

Wednesday

Do Not Doubt What You Pray For

²⁰He replied, 'Because you have so little faith. Truly I tell you, if you have faith as small as a mustard seed, you can say to this mountain, "Move from here to there," and it will move. Nothing will be impossible for you.'

Matthew 17:20 NIV

The mustard seed itself may be small, but it grows into a tree with branches large enough for birds to perch in (Matthew 13:32). It is no mistake that Jesus used this as the basis for his parable on faith. With even the smallest amount of belief in the power of Jesus Christ, nothing is impossible for believers to accomplish. When we pray, therefore—and if our prayers are aligned with the Word and will of God—we should never doubt the outcome. Not only will Jesus answer our prayers, but He will also do so more abundantly than we could ever imagine.

WEEK THIRTY-ONE

Sunday

Be Swift To Hear, Slow To Speak, And Slower Still To Anger

¹⁹My dear brothers and sisters, take note of this: Everyone should be quick to listen, slow to speak and slow to become angry, ²⁰because human anger does not produce the righteousness that God desires. ²¹Therefore, get rid of all moral filth and the evil that is so prevalent and humbly accept the word planted in you, which can save you.

²²Do not merely listen to the word, and so deceive yourselves. Do what it says.

James 1:19-22 NIV

God loves us so much that He has not only saved us from the power of sin and death, but also—though His living Word—has given us instructions concerning how we are meant to live for Him. According to Scripture, we should be more willing to listen when others want to speak to us than to make ourselves heard above them. This is especially true when conflict arises in our relationships. During such times, it is understandable that we may want to voice our grievances or explain how someone else may have hurt us. If we are to live as Christ lived, however, we must let others do the same. In fact, we actually must humble ourselves and allow them to do so first; we must then honestly reflect on what they share with us. If we will faithfully look at things from the perspective of others first, we will find that we will also be slower to upset because we will be responding to them out love rather than ego. God sees everything that we do and hears everything that we say. Let us, therefore, take heed of His instructions so we may honor Him with our lives.

Wednesday

God Made Everything

¹This is what the LORD says:
   'Heaven is my throne,
and the earth is my footstool.
   Where is the house you will build for me?
Where will my resting place be?
   ²Has not my hand made all these things,
and so they came into being?'
   declares the LORD.

Isaiah 66:1-2 NIV

People sometimes like to brag about what they have accomplished in their lives. Even believers are guilty of this at times, especially when they boast about the things they may have done for God. When we do this, however, we are putting our focus on the wrong things. The fact of the matter is that God made everything. When we wake up and look in the mirror, we see faces made in God's image. Everything we have, He has granted us and every action we take, He has enabled us to perform. We are nothing—and we can do nothing—apart from Him. Amazingly, however, God wants to use us in His service despite this. We should seek Him, listen to His commands, and allow Him to lead us where He chooses. Let us then boast about Him.

WEEK THIRTY-TWO

Sunday

Obedience To God

¹⁶So I say, walk by the Spirit, and you will not gratify the desires of the flesh. ¹⁷For the flesh desires what is contrary to the Spirit, and the Spirit what is contrary to the flesh. They are in conflict with each other, so that you are not to do whatever you want. ¹⁸But if you are led by the Spirit, you are not under the law.

Galatians 5:16-17 NIV

Obeying God is one of the most important expressions of worship we can render unto Him. Placing our trust in Him, no matter what the circumstances may be or how nervous they may make us, honors and pleases Him greatly. By contrast, of course, our disobedience—our insistence on doing things our way—displeases God. Surrendering to our flesh and allowing it to rule over the Spirit of God within us can only bring suffering into our lives. God has granted us free will, He has given us the freedom to make our own decisions. Let us, therefore, honor Him by choosing to obey rather than disobey His commands.

Wednesday

Your Assignment

[10]For we must all appear before the judgment seat of Christ, so that each of us may receive what is due us for the things done while in the body, whether good or bad.

2 Corinthians 5:10 NIV

We have all been created by God Almighty, and we all have a part to play in His divine plan. We, as believers, are His instrument upon this earth, His voice to proclaim the Good News of Jesus Christ all across the globe. The devil, of course, would like nothing more than to see us fail in this task, and he will do everything in his power to stop us on a daily basis. We must stand together, encouraging one another and keeping one another uplifted in prayer, if we are to succeed. More importantly, we must speak and act according to the will of God with the power and authority Jesus Christ has bestowed upon us. The assignment we have been given in not one that we can take lightly; it is not one that we can fail to complete. One day we will be judged for the service we have performed in God's name—or the lack thereof. Let us be judged for being faithful servants who advanced His kingdom rather than be condemned for attempting to hold it back.

WEEK THIRTY-THREE

Sunday

Let Peace Rule

²⁷Peace I leave with you; my peace I give you. I do not give to you as the world gives. Do not let your hearts be troubled and do not be afraid.

John 14:27 NIV

For those who are still enslaved to the ways of the world, peace is always a temporary thing. It may be present for a moment, but it always fades away when trouble rears its head. The peace believers experience, however, comes from Jesus Christ. It is perfect, complete, and lasting—the only true peace we can ever know. When we do not have peace in our lives, we cannot do anything worthwhile—either for ourselves or for God. Let us, therefore, seek the peace that surpasses human understanding (Philippians 4:7), for only then will be able to hear and respond to the voice of God.

Wednesday

The Power Of Life Or Death

²¹The tongue has the power of life and death,
and those who love it will eat its fruit.
Proverb 18:21 NIV

When the Lord created all things, He did so with His words. God spoke, commanding the universe and all things within it to take shape, and they did so. Mankind has been made in His image. Just as His words are powerful, so are ours. We can either heal or wound others with our speech. As believers, let us take care that our words are soft and encouraging rather than sharp and harmful. We will all one day eat the fruit of our labors. Let us make sure that it is the sweet fruit of the Spirit rather than the rotten fruit of the world.

WEEK THIRTY-FOUR

Sunday

Trust In God Alone

⁸It is better to take refuge in the LORD
THAN TO TRUST IN HUMANS.
⁹It is better to take refuge in the LORD
than to trust in princes.

Psalm 118:8-9 NIV

When God promises something—whether it is reward or correction—He delivers. He loves us, and every action He takes on our behalf stems from that love. Because of this, He will always faithfully keep His word to us. The same thing cannot be said of mankind. Most of the people we come into contact with act according to their own motives; they are rarely loving or focused on the well-being of others. In fact, people often work to earn our trust only until they get what they need from us. Others may not act so selfishly, but they still often break their word—even unintentionally—because circumstances overwhelm them. This can only lead to disappointment and, if we are not careful, disillusion. Given these two realities, it only makes sense to trust in God above man. He, unlike other people we may know, will never let us down.

Wednesday

Grace

⁶And God raised us up with Christ and seated us with him in the heavenly realms in Christ Jesus, ⁷in order that in the coming ages he might show the incomparable riches of his grace, expressed in his kindness to us in Christ Jesus. ⁸For it is by grace you have been saved, through faith—and this is not from yourselves, it is the gift of God—⁹not by works, so that no one can boast. ¹⁰For we are God's handiwork, created in Christ Jesus to do good works, which God prepared in advance for us to do.

Ephesians 2:6-10 NIV

Some people wrongly teach that if we do enough good deeds, we can somehow earn God's favor. These are the same people who also teach that if we do more good deeds than bad, we can earn our way into Heaven. Scripture, however, tells us that we are saved by the grace of God. Grace—God's undeserved and immeasurable favor upon mankind—is not something we should take lightly. He bestowed it upon us before we were born and granted us life; He daily continues to bestow it upon us by delaying His judgment so that we may come to Him through His Son, Jesus Christ. Every blessing we receive, every punishment we are spared, every word of correction we are given is an example of God's continued grace. We cannot earn it and we do not deserve it, and that is what makes it so amazing. The grace of God covers each one of us—believers and non-believers, alike—every single day. That is how much He loves us.

WEEK THIRTY-FIVE

Sunday

Your Life Is A Fleeting One

*⁴'Show me, L*ORD*, my life's end*
and the number of my days;
let me know how fleeting my life is.

Psalm 39:4 NIV

Compared to the vastness of eternity, we are on this earth for only a very short period of time. This is why it is so important that we respond immediately when God speaks to us. We were not created by God only to live and die; He created each one of us for a reason. Each of us has a purpose in His divine plan. Whether it is to preach the Good News, to minister to the needy, to encourage the downtrodden, or to serve the poor, each of us has a unique task to perform for God in the time He has given us. No one knows how much time he or she may have remaining. No one, therefore, has any time to waste. We must heed the voice of God and obey His commands as soon as we hear Him speak. He will direct us where He needs us and fill us with the power to do what He expects of us as well.

Wednesday

Strengthen Your Brothers And Sisters

[1]Brothers and sisters, if someone is caught in a sin, you who live by the Spirit should restore that person gently.

Galatians 6:1 NIV

As members of the body of Christ, we are expected to speak and act according to the fruit of the Holy Spirit within us (Galatians 5:22-23). As human beings, however, we still struggle against our flesh. At times we will fail to live as we should. This is precisely why God has given us so many brothers and sister in the faith—so they can gently help us see how our behavior displeases God and guide us back to His path. God knows we will stumble at times, and He has made allowance for this by providing us with a family that encompasses the entire world. No matter where we go, we will never be alone. We will always have others we can turn to for encouragement and strength.

WEEK THIRTY-SIX

Sunday

Walk With Boldness

[19] Pray also for me, that whenever I speak, words may be given me so that I will fearlessly make known the mystery of the gospel, [20] for which I am an ambassador in chains. Pray that I may declare it fearlessly, as I should.

Ephesians 6:19-20 NIV

Walking as Jesus did is not an easy task. Despite our love and compassion for them, there are some in the world who will hate us for proclaiming the Word of God. Some people may try to hinder our efforts; still others may seek to do us harm. We cannot let this frighten us, however, nor make us timid in our service. Our Heavenly Father has granted us His authority to serve in the advancement of His kingdom. As we come to rely on Him more and more for the guidance and strength to do so, we will find that our boldness will grow as well.

Wednesday

The Faith Of A Believer

⁶And without faith it is impossible to please God, because anyone who comes to him must believe that he exists and that he rewards those who earnestly seek him.

Hebrews 11:6 NIV

Faith is much more than just believing God exists. Even the devil and his demons believe in God (James 2:19), but they are not creatures of faith. The faith of a believer not only involves believing that God exists, but also that God came to earth in the person of Jesus Christ and that Jesus died as a sacrifice for our sin so that we may have eternal life. Faith also involves absolute confidence that the Word of God is true. Without such faith a person can never truly enter into a relationship with Jesus Christ—can never receive the salvation He offers—no matter what he or she professes to believe.

WEEK THIRTY-SEVEN

Sunday

The Poor

¹⁶ This is how we know what love is: Jesus Christ laid down his life for us. And we ought to lay down our lives for our brothers and sisters. ¹⁷ If anyone has material possessions and sees a brother or sister in need but has no pity on them, how can the love of God be in that person?
1 John 3:16-17 NIV

It is be difficult to imagine what the life of a truly impoverished person must be like. There are, after all, some people who literally have nothing other than the clothes on their backs, people who must eat out of the trash if they want to eat at all. Society often turns a blind eye to people like this because it is easier to pretend that they do not exist than to help them. God is not like society, however; throughout His Word, He instructs us to provide for the poor and demonstrates multiple ways we can do so. Jesus abandoned the glory of Heaven and came to earth in order to save us (Philippians 2:6-8). The very least we can do is sacrifice some of the wealth He has bestowed upon us and serve others in His name as He has commanded.

Wednesday

Power To Live

¹Therefore, there is now no condemnation for those who are in Christ Jesus, ²because through Christ Jesus the law of the Spirit who gives life has set you free from the law of sin and death. ³For what the law was powerless to do because it was weakened by the flesh, God did by sending his own Son in the likeness of sinful flesh to be a sin offering. And so he condemned sin in the flesh, ⁴in order that the righteous requirement of the law might be fully met in us, who do not live according to the flesh but according to the Spirit.

Romans 8:1-4 NIV

In a sense, we are like spiritual batteries. As long as we are connected to Jesus Christ, we will have the energy and strength to serve God in whatever capacity He commands us. When we disconnect ourselves from Jesus, however, eventually we wear down and become ineffective. There is no good thing to be found in the flesh (Romans 7:18), so there is no alternate source of power we can turn to. We must, therefore, cling to Jesus and allow Him to give us the power we need to live in accordance with His will.

WEEK THIRTY-EIGHT

Sunday

Come To Jesus

²⁸Come to me, all you who are weary and burdened, and I will give you rest. ²⁹Take my yoke upon you and learn from me, for I am gentle and humble in heart, and you will find rest for your souls. ³⁰For my yoke is easy and my burden is light.

Matthew 11:28-30 NIV

Without the Lord, life is full of misery. A person may escape his or her suffering for a time, but ultimately it will return. The guilt and shame associated with sin are simply too great to bear. When we come to know Jesus, however, everything changes. We stop being slaves to sin and instead become bondservants of the Lord; the burden of sin is replaced by the joy of service. This does not mean our lives suddenly become problem-free, but because Jesus walks with us and carries us when we lack the strength to carry on under our own power, whatever problems we do face become significantly less overwhelming. In Jesus we find rest because all of our worldly burdens remain at the foot of His cross.

Wednesday

Living Sacrifices

¹Therefore, I urge you, brothers and sisters, in view of God's mercy, to offer your bodies as a living sacrifice, holy and pleasing to God—this is your true and proper worship.

Romans 12:1 NIV

When a person really desires something, he or she will do almost anything to see that desire fulfilled. If that person is enslaved to the ways of the world, all of his or her efforts will be vainly spent pursuing things that can never bring lasting happiness. A person who has surrendered his or her life to God, however, can do better. The same energy he or she once devoted to pursuing worldly things can instead be devoted to those that are Godly. If we are sincere in our faith, this is exactly what we will seek to do.

WEEK THIRTY-NINE

Sunday

The Believer's Prayer Life

¹I urge, then, first of all, that petitions, prayers, intercession and thanksgiving be made for all people—²for kings and all those in authority, that we may live peaceful and quiet lives in all godliness and holiness. ³This is good, and pleases God our Savior, ⁴who wants all people to be saved and to come to a knowledge of the truth.

1 Timothy 2:1-4 NIV

Many officials in our government say they are believers, but the laws and policies they promote are often contrary to the Word of God. We do not have to like or agree with their political views, but because the Lord calls us to love these people as He loves them, we must still devote time to praying for them. They are the leaders of our nation. The only way they will ever be able to act in accordance with the wisdom of the Lord is if they first see the light of His Son, Jesus Christ. As believers, this should be what we pray for on their behalf.

Wednesday

Resurrection And Life

[25]*Jesus said to her, 'I am the resurrection and the life. The one who believes in me will live, even though they die;* [26]*and whoever lives by believing in me will never die. Do you believe this?'*

John 11:25-26 NIV

Very few people—if anyone—can say that they know someone who has never told a lie. Even if it was just a "white lie" meant to spare someone's feelings, we are all guilty of saying something that has been untrue. Only Jesus is without sin; only His words can always be believed. We can rest assured that whatever promises He has made to us, He will keep. He is the Door to eternal life with God. If we will only place our faith in Him, the Door will be opened to us forever.

WEEK FORTY

Sunday

Delight In The Lord

¹Blessed is the one
who does not walk in step with the wicked
or stand in the way that sinners take
or sit in the company of mockers,
²but whose delight is in the law of the LORD,
and who meditates on his law day and night.
³That person is like a tree planted by streams of water,
which yields its fruit in season
and whose leaf does not wither—
whatever they do prospers.

Psalm 1:1-3 NIV

There is no shortage of opinions in the world today. Whether they give it freely or expect some type of compensation for it, everyone seems to have advice they expect someone else to follow. When we choose to follow the suggestions of those who do not know the Lord, we can be certain only bad things will follow. When we are uncertain or when we entertain doubt, there is only once source of truth we can turn to in order to find direction—the Word of God. Those who trust in God for guidance will only be rewarded for doing so. It is God—and God alone—who makes our paths straight (Proverb 3:6).

Wednesday

The Authority Of Jesus

[18] Then Jesus came to them and said, 'All authority in heaven and on earth has been given to me. [19] Therefore go and make disciples of all nations, baptizing them in the name of the Father and of the Son and of the Holy Spirit, [20] and teaching them to obey everything I have commanded you. And surely I am with you always, to the very end of the age.'

Matthew 28:18-20 NIV

Each and every person on earth is imperfect; at some point or another, everyone makes a bad decision or acts on bad advice. Only Jesus has all the power and wisdom of God at His command; only Jesus deserves to be at the center of our lives. Just as He instructed His first followers to make disciples of all the world, so does He instruct us to do the same today. We can rest assured that He will guide us and provide for us in our efforts to do so.

WEEK FORTY-ONE

Sunday

The Holy Spirit Of God

26But the Advocate, the Holy Spirit, whom the Father will send in my name, will teach you all things and will remind you of everything I have said to you.

John 14:26 NIV

Some people think they can gain all the knowledge and understanding they will ever need through books, lectures, online materials, or some other worldly resource. Even believers sometimes fall victim to this mentality. Some well-meaning Christians engage in all manner of Bible study in their efforts to gain deeper understanding of the Word. While their passion may be admirable, it is also misplaced if they attempt to do these things without the prompting of the Holy Spirit. Only the Holy Spirit of God can reveal spiritual truth to us, and He will do so through whatever medium He chooses at the time of His choosing as well. Let us, therefore, seek to be filled with the Spirit at all times so we can receive what He wants to teach us the moment He is ready to do so.

Wednesday

Good Times

[2]*For he says,*
 'In the time of my favor I heard you,
and in the day of salvation I helped you.'
 I tell you, now is the time of God's favor, now is
 the day of salvation.

2 Corinthians 6:2 NIV

Because Christians should be dedicated to living their lives according to the Word of God, some people believe they are prevented from ever being truly happy. What these people do not understand, of course, is that the joy of Christ dwells in the hearts of believers and, as such, obedience and service to the Lord are blessings. Gathering with other believers to serve, fellowship, or worship not only brings great happiness to believers, but also to God. He pours out His favor upon His children, beginning with the day of their salvation and continuing every day thereafter. The joy to be found in that cannot be measured.

WEEK FORTY-TWO

Sunday

Rooted In Christ

⁶So then, just as you received Christ Jesus as Lord, continue to live your lives in him, ⁷rooted and built up in him, strengthened in the faith as you were taught, and overflowing with thankfulness.

Colossians 2:6-7 NIV

The body of Christ has been established to carry the Good News into the world. We, the members of this body, cannot do this if we never step outside the doors of our churches. We may find comfort and strength in the company of other believers, but they are not the individuals who need to hear our message. We must instead enter the wilderness and preach to the lost souls we encounter there. This will be trying at times, and we may experience moments of discouragement, doubt, or even fear. If we remain rooted in Christ, however, and seek our strength through the Word of God, even the difficult moments will seem like blessings for we will be experiencing them in the service of our Lord.

Wednesday

Always Make Yourself Available To God

[20]In a large house there are articles not only of gold and silver, but also of wood and clay; some are for special purposes and some for common use. [21]Those who cleanse themselves from the latter will be instruments for special purposes, made holy, useful to the Master and prepared to do any good work.

2 Timothy 2:20-21 NIV

Although Christians must remain in the world until Jesus returns to claim His church, we are not meant to be a part of it (1 John 2:15-17). This means that while we must love and minister to those who still have not surrendered their lives to Christ, we are not to follow in their ways as we once did. We must separate ourselves from them by living lives that are holy and pure and, in doing so, allow ourselves to be lights that shine for God in an otherwise dark world.

WEEK FORTY-THREE

Sunday

Free Men

²²For the one who was a slave when called to faith in the Lord is the Lord's freed person; similarly, the one who was free when called is Christ's slave. ²³You were bought at a price; do not become slaves of human beings.

1 Corinthians 7:22-23 NIV

Because we live in a fallen world, we are in bondage to sin from the very moment we are born. No man or woman can escape the curse of death it brings through his or her own efforts. Praise be to God, however, that He saw fit to offer us a path of redemption. This did not come without a cost, however; in fact, the price He paid was greater than any other throughout all eternity. Jesus came to earth to live and die for our sin, shedding His blood upon the cross as a final sacrifice that would reconcile us to God. He paid the debt for our transgressions; He set us free. Let us, therefore, set our affections upon Him, repaying His love for us with service to God.

Wednesday

Give As Jesus Gives

[38] Give, and it will be given to you. A good measure, pressed down, shaken together and running over, will be poured into your lap. For with the measure you use, it will be measured to you.

Luke 6:38 NIV

Those who have not yet received Christ into their hearts can never truly understand what it means to freely give unto others. Of course they can share their possessions, but they will always expect something in return. Their acts of giving, like their love, are conditional. This is not how Christ gave when He sacrificed His life for us, nor is it how those who serve Him are to give. Our service unto others is meant to be unconditional, rendered with no expectation of repayment. As much as it is within our power, we are to give unto others that they may be blessed. If we are faithful in this, our Father in Heaven will likewise be faithful and bless us a well.

WEEK FORTY-FOUR

Sunday

Step Out On Faith

37For,
'In just a little while,
he who is coming will come
and will not delay.'
38And,
'But my righteous one will live by faith.
And I take no pleasure
in the one who shrinks back.'

Hebrews 10:37-38 NIV

The Word of God says that the just shall live by faith (Habakkuk 2:4). What this means is that when Christians feel God leading them to act, they are to do just that, even when—especially when—they feel it is something that they cannot actually achieve on their own. Stepping out on faith means taking action despite our doubts or the odds that may be stacked against us. It means trusting that God has a plan and will be with us every step of the way. If Peter stepped out on faith when Jesus called to him and walked on water as a result (Matthew 14:28-29), we, too, can achieve what others say is impossible if we live our faith just as powerfully.

Wednesday

The Cup

⁵You prepare a table before me
in the presence of my enemies.
You anoint my head with oil;
my cup overflows.

Psalm 23:5 NIV

The cup in this verse refers to the life that is promised to every born-again believer who allows him- or herself to be led by the Holy Spirit. The Living Water in this cup will fill us both physically and spiritually when we drink of it, empowering us with the ability to render our daily acts of service unto the Lord. The world will despise us for these acts. No matter what may come our way, however, we will be blessed for the Lord will provide for us at all times and carry us through.

WEEK FORTY-FIVE

Sunday

The Excellence Of The Father

⁵I am the LORD, and there is no other;
apart from me there is no God.

Isaiah 45:5 NIV

Our God is a perfect God, and all of His plans are likewise perfect (Matthew 5:48; Psalm 18:30). As such, He will never mislead us. He is complete in every respect, lacking nothing, the full and absolute embodiment of light, goodness, love, justice, and truth. What is more, He freely bestows these blessings upon His children. That is how much He cares for us, for all of His creation. Our God is awesome, more worthy of praise than anything or anyone else, either in the heavens or on earth (Psalm 145:3). Granting Him honor through daily worship and devotion should be the task of every man, woman, and child who call themselves believers.

Wednesday

The Excellence Of The Son

³⁶For from him and through him and for him are all things.
To him be the glory forever! Amen.

Romans 11:36 NIV

When we look at the world and consider everything that exists, it quickly becomes obvious that life did not happen by accident. Someone had a plan for all of creation, someone much bigger than you or me, our parents, or anyone else. That person is the Lord Jesus Christ. Through the person and power of Jesus, all things have been made and all things are daily being sustained (Colossians 1:17; Hebrews 1:3). He grants wisdom to those who seek it, and He counsels all who call upon Him to do so. He works all things for the good of those who love Him and seek His ways (Romans 8:28). Because of this, we can safely trust in Him at all times. His love for us has no bounds.

WEEK FORTY-SIX

Sunday

When You Are Tested

⁶In all this you greatly rejoice, though now for a little while you may have had to suffer grief in all kinds of trials. ⁷These have come so that the proven genuineness of your faith—of greater worth than gold, which perishes even though refined by fire—may result in praise, glory and honor when Jesus Christ is revealed. ⁸Though you have not seen him, you love him; and even though you do not see him now, you believe in him and are filled with an inexpressible and glorious joy, ⁹for you are receiving the end result of your faith, the salvation of your souls.

1 Peter 1:6-9 NIV

No one ever said that the Christian life is an easy one to live. In fact, Jesus Himself said exactly the opposite, explaining that those who follow Him will constantly face trouble because the world will hate them for doing so. When we first come to Jesus, we are spiritual babes. We have to grow in our relationship with Him and the knowledge of His Word if we ever hope to mature into spiritual adulthood. This maturity can only be proven if it is tested. There will be many tests throughout our lives, many times when we will be faced with the decision of whether or not to do what we know Jesus would have us do. They will rarely be easy to endure. Fortunately, we can prepare ourselves for them by studying the Word of God. Let us strive to be good students who pass the tests they are given and—through them—grow in wisdom.

Wednesday

A Life Touched By Jesus Is Never The Same

²²You were taught, with regard to your former way of life, to put off your old self, which is being corrupted by its deceitful desires; ²³to be made new in the attitude of your minds; ²⁴and to put on the new self, created to be like God in true righteousness and holiness.

Ephesians 4:22-24 NIV

Once we get a taste of the love of Jesus, we will never be the same. It is impossible for a person to remain unchanged after realizing the Lord of lords and King of kings loved him or her enough to sacrifice Himself, taking the sin of the entire world upon Himself and clothing those who would seek Him in His own perfection. When we come to Him and receive the gift of life that He offers, our hearts of stone become hearts of flesh (Ezekiel 36:26) and our once blind eyes suddenly have their sight restored (Matthew 11:4-5). Not only will we see the world in a different way, our very lifestyles will change as well. What we once loved, we will hate and what we once hated, we will love. The prosperity promised in the Bible is, first and foremost, the prosperity within our hearts. That is where Jesus takes up residence within us; that must also be the source of every decision we make and every action we undertake after He does so.

WEEK FORTY-SEVEN

Sunday

Love Others Like Christ Loves You

¹²My command is this: Love each other as I have loved you.
John 15:12 NIV

We will be judged for everything we do in this life, both by those in the world and—one day—by Jesus as well. The former should not stop us from living according to the Word of God because the latter will give us the power and ability to endure whatever opposition we may face as we do so. Believers are to walk as Jesus walked, talk as Jesus talked, and—above all—love as love as Jesus loved. This means that we must even love our enemies. After all, we were still enemies of God when Jesus poured out His love for us upon the cross (Matthew 5:44; Romans 5:10). We will one day have to give an answer for whatever we are doing right this very moment. Let us, therefore, strive to treat others as we want to be treated, to treat them as Jesus has treated us.

Wednesday

God Is Your Refuge

¹Whoever dwells in the shelter of the Most High
will rest in the shadow of the Almighty.
²I will say of the LORD, 'He is my refuge and my fortress,
my GOD, in whom I trust.'
³Surely he will save you
from the fowler's snare
and from the deadly pestilence.
⁴He will cover you with his feathers,
and under his wings you will find refuge;
his faithfulness will be your shield and rampart.

Psalm 91:1-4 NIV

The modern world is so full of sin, there are times when we all we may want is a place we can run to in order to find peace, strength, hope, or renewal. If we look for such a place anywhere but in the company of God, our search will be in vain. Only God is pure and holy; only in His presence can we find freedom from the evil that is around us. If we turn to God when we are in need, we will never be disappointed. If we put our faith and trust in Him, He will take us in His arms and shelter us from every storm. He is our refuge, and in His loving care we will always find peace.

WEEK FORTY-EIGHT

Sunday

Seek God

¹¹For the LORD GOD is a sun and shield;
the LORD bestows favor and honor;
no good thing does he withhold
from those whose walk is blameless.

Psalm 84:11 NIV

God has given each one of us gifts to use for the advancement of His kingdom. God has placed His own Holy Spirit inside of us so that we can use these gifts for that very purpose. He loves us so deeply that He left the perfection of Heaven and came into the fallen world to save us from sin. He will withhold nothing from us if we earnestly seek Him and ask Him to bless us according to His will. As we grow stronger in our walk with Him, as we seek to be blameless through the power of His Spirit, He will not only reveal His glory to us, but to those He will touch through us as well.

Wednesday

Believe And Receive

[6]But when you pray, go into your room, close the door and pray to your Father, who is unseen. Then your Father, who sees what is done in secret, will reward you. [7]And when you pray, do not keep on babbling like pagans, for they think they will be heard because of their many words. [8]Do not be like them, for your Father knows what you need before you ask him.

Matthew 6:6-8 NIV

The very first person to care for us—the person who cared for us before we were even born—was God. He cared for us enough to not only create us, but also create everything that we will need throughout our lives in order to fulfill His plan for us. Every step we will take in this life, every day of life we have been granted, He has already ordained (Psalm 139:16). In short, God knows everything about us. When we pray, therefore, we can safely trust in God to answer according to our needs because He knows them better than we ourselves do. Let us never fear to go to our secret places and seek Him. He *will* hear us, and He *will* provide.

WEEK FORTY-NINE

Sunday

The Living God

¹³The blood of goats and bulls and the ashes of a heifer sprinkled on those who are ceremonially unclean sanctify them so that they are outwardly clean. ¹⁴How much more, then, will the blood of Christ, who through the eternal Spirit offered himself unblemished to God, cleanse our consciences from acts that lead to death, so that we may serve the living God!

Hebrews 9:13-14 NIV

Many cultures have worshipped gods who were very much like human beings. They were capable of making the same mistakes, fell victim to the same failings, and could be overthrown or killed by other gods who were more powerful. Our God, however, is different. Unlike the gods of other cultures, our God is real and He is far greater than anything He has created. He is all-knowing and all-powerful, able to be everywhere at once while simultaneously dwelling within the heart of each individual believer as well. Everywhere we look, we see evidence of His presence. He has not passed away, but is instead very much at work both in our lives and in the world around us. Through the sacrifice of Jesus, we have been reconciled to God; through the power of the Spirit, we have been empowered to serve Him. As God is alive, so has He made us alive. It is up to us to allow the Spirit of God to flow through us and bring life to others as well.

Wednesday

Love God With All Your Being

28One of the teachers of the law came and heard them debating. Noticing that Jesus had given them a good answer, he asked him, 'Of all the commandments, which is the most important?'

29'The most important one,' answered Jesus, 'is this: "Hear, O Israel: The Lord our God, the Lord is one. 30Love the Lord your God with all your heart and with all your soul and with all your mind and with all your strength."'

Mark 12:28-29 NIV

The love that God has poured out on us is unconditional. We did not earn it nor would He ever expect us to try to do so. If we are loved that much by our Father in Heaven, why would we even consider not loving Him in return? God is love. His very act of creation was an act of love, and all of His created things are meant to act in love as well (1 John 4:8). Above all things, we must love God first. Every bit of our hearts, souls, minds, and strength must be devoted to Him. This is how we must love Him for it is how He first loved us.

WEEK FIFTY

Sunday

Be Transformed

¹Therefore, I urge you, brothers and sisters, in view of God's mercy, to offer your bodies as a living sacrifice, holy and pleasing to God—this is your true and proper worship. ²Do not conform to the pattern of this world, but be transformed by the renewing of your mind. Then you will be able to test and approve what God's will is—his good, pleasing and perfect will.

Romans 12:1-2 NIV

We have all visited places we have previously been—where we were born or where we went to school, for example—and were shocked to see how much they had changed in the years that had passed. This level of transformation is the same type of change that must take place within us when we are born again of the Spirit. Christians are called by that name because they claim to be followers of Jesus Christ. We cannot follow Jesus and maintain a worldview still bound to sin—it simply is not possible. We must instead allow our minds to be transformed through the reading and study of God's word. This is where we gain understanding of God's will. As we allow the Holy Spirit within us to do so, He will first change us, then guide our hearts and minds so we can fulfill it.

Wednesday

God Will Repay

¹⁷Do not repay anyone evil for evil. Be careful to do what is right in the eyes of everyone. ¹⁸If it is possible, as far as it depends on you, live at peace with everyone. ¹⁹Do not take revenge, my dear friends, but leave room for God's wrath, for it is written: 'It is mine to avenge; I will repay,' says the Lord.

Romans 12:17-19 NIV

The world will hate those who choose to follow Jesus and live according to God's Word (Matthew 10:22). Some people will insult and ridicule us, while others may very well try to bring us harm. It is only natural for us to feel an urge to defend ourselves, to pay these people back for the hardships they inflict upon us. That is the very reason why we must avoid doing so. Christians are no longer meant to live according to the rules of the natural world, but rather those of the spiritual realm. Despite what they may do to us, we are to mind our tongues and restrain our actions. We are to love those who hate us and allow God to deal with them instead. He will either use our meek and gentle natures to touch their hearts or He will, in time, repay them for their actions against us. In either case, the battle must remain the Lord's (2 Chronicles 20:15).

WEEK FIFTY-ONE

Sunday

Prayer Is A Lifestyle

⁹For this reason, since the day we heard about you, we have not stopped praying for you. We continually ask God to fill you with the knowledge of his will through all the wisdom and understanding that the Spirit gives, ¹⁰so that you may live a life worthy of the Lord and please him in every way: bearing fruit in every good work, growing in the knowledge of God, ¹¹being strengthened with all power according to his glorious might so that you may have great endurance and patience, ¹²and giving joyful thanks to the Father, who has qualified you to share in the inheritance of his holy people in the kingdom of light.

Colossians 1:9-12 NIV

Prayer is not an action a believer should engage in only when he or she needs help, nor is it something that a believer should struggle to find time to do. Prayer is not an emergency line to God, nor is it a burden. Prayer should instead be part of a believer's lifestyle, and a joy-filled one at that. Prayer changes things—in our lives, in the lives of others, and in the world at large. Jesus prayed unto His Father and countless people were blessed as a result. Believers are all brothers and sisters of Jesus Christ. Our Father in Heaven hears our prayers just as He heard those of Jesus, and He will bless others through us as well.

Wednesday

God's Word Will Never Change

[17] Because God wanted to make the unchanging nature of his purpose very clear to the heirs of what was promised, he confirmed it with an oath. [18] God did this so that, by two unchangeable things in which it is impossible for God to lie, we who have fled to take hold of the hope set before us may be greatly encouraged. [19] We have this hope as an anchor for the soul, firm and secure.

Hebrews 6:17-19 NIV

When God finished His act of creation, He saw all that He had made and declared that it was very good (Genesis 1:31). God then freely gave everything He had made to mankind so it could prosper (Genesis 1:28)—this includes the provision of His Word. In our modern world, people have attempted to justify the sins they refuse to give up by manipulating the Word of God or suggesting that it is no longer valid. They are, of course, mistaken. God is unchanging; Jesus Christ is the same "yesterday and today and forever" (Hebrews 13:8); the Holy Spirit is eternal. The promises the Triune God has made, the laws He has established, and the commands He has given are just as lasting.

WEEK FIFTY-TWO

Sunday

God Loves Us

16For God so loved the world that he gave his one and only Son, that whoever believes in him shall not perish but have eternal life.

John 3:16 NIV

Evidence of God's mercy and grace abound throughout Scripture. Even when we do wrong, even when we stumble and fall, God still loves us enough to forgive us if we ask Him to do so. Though He hates the sin that is in the world, He loves us enough to withhold the day of His wrath until all those who will believe have come to faith (2 Peter 3:9). The Word of God provides us with proof of His intense and boundless love for us so often, it seems inconceivable that anyone could ever doubt it. We have so much to be thankful for. If we are truly going to honor God, we should make time each and every day to lift prayers of thanksgiving to Him in return.

Wednesday

Be A Friend Toward Everyone

[24]One who has unreliable friends soon comes to ruin,
but there is a friend who sticks closer than a brother.
Proverb 18:24 NIV

Throughout our lifetimes, we have relationship with many people we call friends. Some are with us only for a time, while others remain by our side through thick and thin. Although Jesus Christ is the only Friend we can count on one hundred percent, one hundred percent of the time, God brings others into our lives and establishes bonds between us for a reason. We are meant to enjoy fellowship with others and to find strength in the company of those who care about us. We are meant to be a source of strength for others when they are in need as well. We must stick close to those whom God brings into our lives for as long as He allows us to have relationships with them. Friends are a blessing in this life. We should strive to be a friend to everyone we meet and, by doing so, become a blessing to them as well.

INDEX OF SCRIPTURES

AUTHOR'S NOTE

Verses that appear in **bold** print represent quoted Scriptural passages. Verses that appear in non-bold print represent Scriptural references only.

Printed in the United States
by Bookmasters